Original title:
After the Darkness

Copyright © 2024 Swan Charm
All rights reserved.

Author: Eliora Lumiste
ISBN HARDBACK: 978-9916-79-048-9
ISBN PAPERBACK: 978-9916-79-049-6
ISBN EBOOK: 978-9916-79-050-2

A New Day's Muse

A gentle dawn breaks the quiet sky,
With whispers of hope, the night bids goodbye.
Sunlight dances on dew-kissed leaves,
Awakening dreams that the heart weaves.

Birds serenade with their morning song,
The world stirs to life, where we all belong.
Each petal unfurls in colors bold,
A tapestry woven with threads of gold.

The breeze carries secrets of days to unfold,
In the warmth of the sun, all fears are consoled.
Step into the light, let your spirit roam,
For today marks the start of a journey home.

Clouds drift lazily, painting the blue,
A canvas of promise, fresh and anew.
Find solace in moments, both tender and true,
As the dawn breaks forth, revealing what's due.

So breathe in deep, let your heart be free,
Embrace the new day, let it be the key.
In the hush of the morn, find your own way,
As life gathers blooms, in the light of the day.

The Heart's Lament Transformed

In shadows deep, the echoes reside,
A heart made of fragments, where dreams often hide.
Silent whispers of love, lost in the night,
Yet within the darkness, there flickers a light.

Tears trace the path where joy used to flow,
Carrying burdens too heavy to show.
But resilience stirs in the depths of the pain,
For with every chapter, there's growth to regain.

Beneath the weight, the spirit holds strong,
Transforming the sorrow, where we all belong.
From ashes arise the stories untold,
In the warmth of the hearth, let the heart be bold.

Time weaves its magic, stitching the seams,
Turning lament into beautifully bright dreams.
The past finds its place, as the present unfolds,
With love as the anchor, and courage that holds.

So let the heart sing, in vibrant refrain,
For the pain that once was now nurtures the gain.
Embrace transformation, let go of the fear,
As the heart's lament becomes a song clear.

Shattered Chains of Night

In the stillness, shadows play,
Whispers lost in the moonlight's sway.
Dreams unbound, they take to flight,
Breaking free from the chains of night.

Stars fall softly, a silver rain,
Chasing away the echoes of pain.
With each dawn, hope ignites,
Shattered chains, and heart takes flight.

Fingers stretch to grasp the day,
While the night's grip fades away.
In the glow, new paths align,
With every breath, the world will shine.

The darkness fades, it knows its place,
A fleeting ghost, a warm embrace.
In the twilight's hymn, souls delight,
Emerging whole, from shattered night.

Embrace of the Morning

Golden rays kiss the earth anew,
Awakening dreams wrapped in dew.
Birds sing sweetly, a soft refrain,
In the embrace of morning's gain.

Gentle breezes stir the trees,
Whispering secrets with perfect ease.
Colors dance in radiant light,
The world awakens, pure and bright.

Hope is born with each new beam,
Life unfolds like a fleeting dream.
In this moment, all feels right,
Forever held in morning's sight.

With open hearts, we greet the dawn,
Casting shadows of worries gone.
Together we rise, take flight,
In the embrace of morning light.

In the Wake of Twilight

Softly fading, the daylight wanes,
Colors blending in twilight's chains.
Whispers carry on a hushed breeze,
In the wake of night, the world finds ease.

Stars awaken, one by one,
Beneath the glow of the setting sun.
A tranquil hush, the earth takes flight,
In the gentle arms of velvet night.

Mingling hues of blue and gold,
Stories of twilight's grace unfold.
Moments linger, hearts unite,
In the sanctum of fading light.

Dreamers roam where shadows weave,
In the beauty of night, we believe.
With every breath, we hold on tight,
In the wake of twilight's flight.

Journey Toward the Sun

With each step, the horizon calls,
Where hope flows free and courage sprawls.
Across the valleys, through the trees,
We journey onward, guided by breeze.

Chasing shadows, leaving fear,
The path ahead is crystal clear.
In our hearts, the fire burns,
With every twist, the world returns.

Mountains rise, and rivers gleam,
Fueled by faith, we push and dream.
In our souls, the warmth will rise,
Journeying forth to brighter skies.

With open arms, we greet the dawn,
Through trials faced, our spirits drawn.
In each moment, we become one,
On our journey, toward the sun.

Wings of Transformation

In shadows deep, a whisper grows,
A spark ignites, the courage flows.
From silent earth, new life will spring,
With open hearts, we learn to sing.

The world transforms, each soul a flame,
As dreams take flight, we rise, untame.
With every step, the past we free,
Wings unfold in harmony.

From darkened nights to golden dawn,
We weave the threads, the old moves on.
In unity, our voices blend,
A journey shared, a promise penned.

With every turn, a chance to grow,
We paint our skies in vibrant glow.
Together we will dare to soar,
On wings of change, forevermore.

From Ashen Dreams

In twilight's grip, the embers sigh,
They cradle tales of days gone by.
From ashes cold, new fires ignite,
In whispered hopes, we find our light.

The past, a shadow gently fades,
While future blooms in fresh cascades.
With every breath, we rise anew,
The heart ignites, our vision true.

Among the ruins, life takes hold,
In fractured dreams, a story told.
With courage born from deepest fears,
We cherish now, embrace the years.

From ashen dreams, we dance with grace,
In every tear, a warm embrace.
With open hands, we shape our fate,
Together strong, we celebrate.

Glimmers of Reconciliation

In distant lands, where silence grew,
Two hearts converge, with hope anew.
In fragile bonds, we find our way,
To heal the wounds of yesterday.

With gentle hands, we mend the seams,
In quiet whispers, we share dreams.
Through stormy tides, we sail as one,
Beneath the stars, the past undone.

The light of dawn breaks through the haze,
As souls entwine in soft, warm rays.
With every step, we bridge the gap,
In love's embrace, the world unwraps.

A tapestry of hope unfurls,
In woven threads, our peace swirls.
Together, hand in hand we stand,
To dance in light across the land.

A Tapestry of Revival

In colors bold, our stories blend,
Each thread a truth that we defend.
With every stitch, we sew the seams,
A vibrant dance, a thousand dreams.

From quiet past, the present spins,
In harmony, the journey begins.
With every heartbeat, life unfolds,
A dream of warmth, a tale retold.

Across the fabric, time moves fast,
Embracing moments, holding fast.
With laughter echoes, love's embrace,
In every hue, we find our place.

From whispers soft to roars of joy,
We craft the canvas, girl and boy.
In unity, we rise, revive,
A tapestry of hope alive.

Rebirth of the Day

The dawn breaks soft and fair,
With colors that dance in the air.
Awakening nature's sweet sound,
As life unfolds all around.

Sunlight spills through the trees,
Whispers carried by the breeze.
Birds sing their radiant song,
Celebrating where they belong.

Petals open to greet the light,
Chasing away shadows of night.
Each moment a brand new start,
Rebirth felt deep in the heart.

Clouds drift lazily away,
As warmth begins to play.
The world dons a golden hue,
In this canvas, fresh and new.

Life emerges from the night,
In waves of gentle light.
Hope blooms with the day anew,
Rebirth, a gift for me and you.

When Night Surrenders

When night surrenders to the dawn,
Stars fade, dreams are nearly gone.
Silence breaks with morning's breath,
A promise of life, no death.

The moon bids a soft goodbye,
As the sun begins to rise high.
Shadows retreat, taking flight,
Welcoming the warmth of light.

The sky blushes with golden hues,
Wrapped in nature's bright clues.
Each ray whispers tales of time,
Singing sweet like a rhyme.

Crickets hush, their songs now done,
It's time to greet the day, my son.
Awake to wonders that unfold,
In the arms of morning's gold.

With every heartbeat, life returns,
In the glow, our passion burns.
When night surrenders, hold on tight,
For dreams are reborn with the light.

Awakened by Radiance

Awakened by radiance, the world transforms,
Bathed in light, as nature warms.
Gentle whispers in the air,
Promise adventures everywhere.

Morning dew glistens on the grass,
Moments fleeting, yet they last.
Chasing shadows, the sun climbs high,
Painting colors across the sky.

The stillness breaks with joyful cheer,
While creatures stir, drawing near.
Nature's symphony fills the day,
Awakening dreams in every way.

Clouds drift softly, pure and white,
As day unfolds from night.
Each bloom reveals a story old,
Awakened beauty, bright and bold.

Through the branches, light cascades,
Life's vibrance softly parades.
Awakened hearts in joyful praise,
Bask in the warmth, let spirits raise.

The Horizon Awaits

The horizon awaits with open arms,
Embracing dreams and all its charms.
Waves crash softly on the shore,
Inviting us to explore.

Sunsets paint the evening sky,
As day whispers a sweet goodbye.
Horizons stretch, a boundless quest,
A promise held within each crest.

Mountains rise, bold and steep,
Guarding secrets they keep.
Footsteps echo on the ground,
As new adventures abound.

The colors of the dusk ignite,
Field and forest bathed in light.
With each step, we cross the line,
Into a realm where dreams align.

The stars emerge to guide our way,
As night transforms the day.
The horizon calls, an endless span,
A journey waits for every man.

Fragments of the Unseen

In shadows cast by ancient trees,
Whispers dance on the evening breeze.
Secrets lie in the stillness felt,
Stories waiting, yet to be dealt.

Beneath the surface, a world unknown,
Fragments shimmer like precious stone.
Glimmers of truth in the twilight glow,
Paths unfold where few dare to go.

Each moment captured, a fleeting thread,
A tapestry woven where dreams are fed.
Unseen magic in the quiet night,
Hopes align with the dawn's first light.

The heart remembers, though time may fade,
In every silence, a promise made.
Fragments linger in whispers and sighs,
Boundless stories where mystery lies.

Together we walk through the shadows long,
Finding our voices in a forgotten song.
Each fragment cherished, each moment shared,
A dance of the unseen, forever bared.

Threads of Resilience

In the fabric of life, we weave our dreams,
Stitching together the frayed seams.
Each thread a story, a battle fought,
A tapestry rich with lessons taught.

Through stormy nights and dawn's embrace,
We rise with strength, we find our place.
Threads intertwine in a colorful hue,
Resilient hearts, ever bold and true.

With every tear, a chance to mend,
In brokenness, we find our blend.
Woven together, hand in hand,
A chorus of hope in this vast land.

Through trials faced and fears unkind,
The threads of courage we always find.
In moments dark, we gather light,
Resilience blooms, a glorious sight.

Together we stand, forever strong,
In the dance of life, we all belong.
Threads of resilience in unity form,
A tapestry bright that can weather the storm.

Sunlit Promises

Dawn breaks softly on the waking earth,
A golden glow, a moment of birth.
Sunlit promises in the morning air,
Whispers of hope, beyond all despair.

The sky awakens in shades of gold,
Stories of courage and love retold.
Each ray of light a gentle embrace,
Guiding our steps through time and space.

In fields of dreams, we dance and play,
Chasing the shadows that melt away.
Sunlit laughter, a melody sweet,
In every heartbeat, a rhythm, a beat.

The world ignites with a vibrant spark,
Chasing away the remnants of dark.
Promises whispered in every new dawn,
Together we flourish, forever reborn.

As twilight falls, we hold on tight,
To sunlit promises that shine so bright.
In the tapestry of life, we find our way,
Guided by love, each and every day.

Serenity After Strife

In the stillness that follows the storm,
Peace descends, a welcoming warm.
Gentle whispers in the quiet night,
Serenity blooms under soft moonlight.

The echoes of struggle begin to fade,
In the heart's quiet, solace is laid.
Fragile moments of sweet release,
Breathing deeply, we find our peace.

With every heartbeat, we learn to forgive,
In the shadows of strife, we truly live.
Finding strength in the lessons learned,
Through the ashes, a new fire burned.

As dawn approaches with colors anew,
We rise from the pain, refreshed and true.
Serenity whispers, a tender guide,
Through valleys deep, where fears once lied.

Together we walk, hand in hand,
In the garden of life, where we take our stand.
Serenity after strife, a grace to embrace,
A journey of healing, a beautiful place.

Emerging from Shadows

In the quiet hour of night,
Whispers of hope take flight.
Stars peek through the dark veil,
While shadows begin to pale.

Footsteps tread on the ground,
Awakening dreams unbound.
Courage blooms where fear once lay,
Guiding the heart's shy sway.

Hues of dawn paint the sky,
As darkness starts to die.
With each moment, light unfurls,
A new day's promise swirls.

Chains of the past break free,
Embracing who we can be.
From the depths we rise anew,
With spirits bright, bold, and true.

Listen to the song it sings,
Nature's pulse, the joy it brings.
Emerging, we claim our place,
In the sunlight's warm embrace.

Light's Soft Embrace

In the early morn, so sweet,
Golden rays across our feet.
Gentle warmth wraps us tight,
Softly chasing away the night.

Nature stirs in slow delight,
Birds take wing, taking flight.
Sunbeams dance on dew-kissed grass,
In this moment, time does pass.

A breeze whispers through the trees,
Carrying secrets on the breeze.
Flowers bloom, their colors bright,
In the tender touch of light.

Shadows fade in the sun's gaze,
Heart and spirit set ablaze.
Every creature stirs awake,
In this warmth, all fear can break.

Together, we share this grace,
Life's journey in light's embrace.
Hand in hand, we forward tread,
With wishes and dreams widespread.

Dawn's Whispering Light

As the night drifts away,
Softly comes a brand new day.
Luminous hues spread wide,
As darkness takes its stride.

Gentle whispers fill the air,
Promises of joy and care.
Each ray tells a story new,
Painting skies in vibrant hue.

The world stirs from slumber's grasp,
In nature's rhythm, hearts clasp.
Awakening dreams so bright,
In the glow of morning light.

Clouds part to reveal the sun,
Every moment has begun.
With each heartbeat, we arise,
Chasing hope beneath the skies.

Dawn's embrace, a sacred space,
Inviting all with gentle grace.
Through the veil of night we see,
The dawn's light sets us free.

Beyond the Veil

What lies waiting, hidden deep,
Secrets that the shadows keep.
Through the mist, a soft refrain,
Calling souls to break the chain.

Veils of doubt begin to lift,
Revealing life's most precious gift.
Journey forth, do not delay,
Light and love will lead the way.

Listen close, the whisper calls,
In the silence, courage thralls.
Beyond the veil, a world unfolds,
In colors bright, in stories told.

With each step, the heart expands,
Bridging dreams with open hands.
In the glow, the truth ignites,
Illuminating starry nights.

So venture forth, let fear dissolve,
In unity, we can evolve.
Beneath the veil, we claim our place,
In the light's warm, fierce embrace.

Whispers of Dawn

The sky blushes soft and bright,
Birds sing of the coming light.
In the hush, dreams start to sway,
Hope awakens with the day.

Golden rays stretch and unfold,
Chasing night, turning bold.
The world stirs, a breath is drawn,
Embraced by whispers of dawn.

Flowers bloom in warm embrace,
Nature's dance, a gentle grace.
Every petal, kissed by dew,
A canvas painted fresh and new.

Soft winds carry scents divine,
Morning's promise, sweet and fine.
Each heartbeat finds its place,
In the stillness of dawn's chase.

Eyes now open, spirits rise,
Underneath the painted skies.
A tapestry of peace and thrall,
The magic found in the call.

Emergence from the Shadows

In the depths where silence sleeps,
A dance of shapes, a secret keeps.
Whispers curled in shadows tight,
Awaiting for the break of light.

Figures shift, then start to sway,
Cloaked in night, they find their way.
With each pulse, a story spun,
Emergence heralds the rising sun.

Faces soft, yet eyes aflame,
In the dark, they call your name.
From the gloom, they step with care,
Letting go of silent despair.

Every heartbeat breaks the night,
Transforming shadows into light.
With the dawn, they start to rise,
Emerging, bold, beneath the skies.

Once concealed, now fierce and true,
The strength of many breaking through.
In unity, their spirits dance,
In freedom's arms, they claim a chance.

Beneath a Moonlit Veil

Under the shimmer of the moon,
Nights whisper their ancient tune.
Stars wrapped in silver lace,
Time slows in this sacred space.

Shadows play along the ground,
In their depths, secrets are found.
Hearts entwined, a gentle sigh,
Underneath the vast night sky.

The world sleeps, yet dreams awaken,
Promises made, never shaken.
Softly glimmers, the evening's grace,
Hope finds solace in this place.

With every beam that touches skin,
The night's magic starts to spin.
In this moment, lost we stay,
Beneath a moonlit, guiding sway.

Echoes of love, softly told,
In the coolness, we behold.
Wrapped in shadows, hearts reveal,
A connection deep, beneath this veil.

The Light's Gentle Touch

A soft glow breaks the quiet hour,
Whispers warmth, the sun's sweet power.
Each golden ray, a tender brush,
In its presence, worries hush.

Beneath the sky, vast and wide,
Nature dances, hearts open wide.
Every leaf, bathed in delight,
Finding solace in the light.

Moments linger, softly bound,
In the shadows, joy is found.
A tapestry of soft embrace,
In the light's gentle, glowing grace.

With each dawn, renewal speaks,
Restoration as the day peaks.
A canvas of hope, firm and bright,
Held tightly in the light's soft bite.

So let us chase the fleeting beams,
Finding strength in tender dreams.
With open hearts, we rise anew,
In the light's gentle touch, we grew.

The Gathered Radiance

In the calm of dawn's embrace,
Light spills softly, a gentle trace.
Whispers of hope in the dew,
They gather dreams, shining anew.

Colors burst forth, pure delight,
Nature awakens, it takes flight.
Each petal unfurls, a joyful song,
In this moment, where we belong.

The sun climbs high, igniting the skies,
Bringing warmth where the heart lies.
Golden rays dance on the stream,
Holding close our every dream.

Leaves shimmer with a vibrant glow,
Embracing the day, let happiness flow.
In togetherness, we stand tall,
Under the radiance, we rise, we call.

As dusk walks in, colors concede,
We find peace in this gathered creed.
Within the light, our spirits soar,
Ready to greet each day once more.

Wings to the Morning

Awakened by the golden light,
Morning whispers, taking flight.
Birds sing soft, their songs alive,
In search of dreams, let us strive.

The sky paints hues of dusk and dawn,
Starting fresh, like the new-born.
With every breath, the day unfolds,
Stories waiting to be told.

Gentle winds carry hopes afar,
Guiding hearts toward every star.
With open wings, we rise, we soar,
Embracing what this day has in store.

Sunlight dances on fields of gold,
Whispers of nature, a tale retold.
Each moment, we weave our flight,
To chase the dreams that feel so right.

As shadows stretch beneath the trees,
We find our strength in every breeze.
The morning's song, a sweet refrain,
Echoes softly, love will remain.

Emancipation of the Mind

Chains of doubt begin to break,
With every thought, new paths we make.
The freedom to dream, to visualize,
Awakens the soul, uncovers the skies.

Ideas dance like leaves in the breeze,
Delightfully flowing, bringing us ease.
Unfurling the stories within our hearts,
Every syllable a journey that starts.

We dive deep into realms uncharted,
Where wisdom flows and fear has departed.
In silence, we find our light,
Guided by stars, so bold, so bright.

Thoughts become wings, lifting us high,
In this vast expanse, we learn to fly.
Breaking the limits, releasing the binds,
This is the dawn of our free minds.

With every breath, we rise anew,
Exploring visions, pure and true.
The mind, unchained, begins to shine,
In this dance of liberation, we redefine.

Chasing Sunbeams

In golden glimmers, soft and warm,
We chase the sun, away from harm.
With laughter echoing in the air,
Each radiant ray a joyful flare.

Fields of dreams, we dash along,
Heartbeats racing, a vibrant song.
Footsteps light, like whispers shared,
A world of wonder, fully prepared.

Hand in hand, we leap and run,
Spinning laughter in the sun.
Chasing dreams where memories gleam,
In every moment, we find our theme.

The horizon glows with endless grace,
Tracing patterns, we quicken our pace.
Following beams that guide our way,
In the warmth of light, we choose to stay.

As twilight falls and colors blend,
We cherish the day, the joy we send.
In chasing sunbeams, our spirits soar,
Grateful for light, forevermore.

Reawakening the Dreamscape

In whispers soft, the night gives way,
To glimmers bright, where shadows play.
The heart ignites with fervent light,
As dreams arise and take their flight.

The stars align, a cosmic dance,
Illuminating every chance.
With every breath, possibilities bloom,
In this enchanted, vivid room.

With open arms, I embrace the dawn,
Where hope is reborn and fears are gone.
Each moment, a canvas yet to write,
The dreamscape vast, a pure delight.

Through misty paths, I wander free,
In realms where all my dreams can be.
Every vision, a thread of grace,
In this sacred, serene space.

As sunlight breaks the veil of night,
Awakening aspirations bright.
With joy and love, I rise and soar,
In the dreamscape, forevermore.

Veil of the Breaking Dawn

The horizon softly stirs awake,
A blush of gold, the earth to shake.
Each ray of sun, a tender sigh,
As night retreats, the shadows die.

Clouds float gently, a canvas fair,
Whispers of hope fill the air.
The world anew, with promise gleams,
Wrapped in the warmth of morning dreams.

With every step, the day unfolds,
A story bright, in colors bold.
Moments dance in blissful grace,
As life awakens in this space.

The birds sing sweet, a lilting tune,
As flowers bloom beneath the moon.
In this embrace, I find my peace,
A gentle pause, my soul's release.

Through the veil of dawn, I find my way,
To cherish life, come what may.
With every heartbeat, I belong,
In the morning's light, I grow strong.

Gossamer Threads of Tomorrow

In twilight's grace, the whispers start,
Threads of dreams weave through the heart.
Each glimmer bright, a future unseen,
In fragile hope, we chase the green.

Through mazes of thought, I wander wide,
With every step, the world's my guide.
A tapestry spun from wishes bold,
Of stories yet to be told.

With nimble fingers, I grasp the light,
The gossamer strands that shimmer bright.
In every moment, chances sing,
A melody of what dawn may bring.

As shadows dance in the fading sun,
I gather dreams, the race begun.
From fragile threads, we'll build the whole,
A future bright, a soaring soul.

With wings of faith, we rise and shine,
Embracing all that is divine.
Intertwined in love's sweet flow,
We navigate the paths we'll go.

The Resilient Blossom

In garden rich, where colors sway,
A blossom blooms, despite decay.
Through rain and storm, it finds its way,
A testament of strength each day.

With petals soft, and roots held tight,
It faces dark, embracing light.
In every struggle, growth unfolds,
A story of courage that it holds.

As seasons shift, and winds may howl,
The blossom stands, with grace, a prowl.
In vibrant hues, it claims its ground,
A beauty deep, profoundly found.

From cracks of earth, it takes its stance,
A celebration of life, a dance.
Through trials faced, it stands so tall,
A resilient spirit that will not fall.

In every petal, a tale is spun,
Of hope and strength, of battles won.
With gentle whispers, it calls to me,
To nurture dreams, to simply be.

Rebirth of the Starry Night

In darkness deep, the stars awake,
They shimmer bright, as dreams they make.
A canvas rich with tales untold,
The night unfolds, both brave and bold.

With whispers soft, the cosmos calls,
As nightingale in silence falls.
The moonlit dance, a guiding spark,
Reviving hopes within the dark.

Each twinkling light, a secret shared,
A testament of all who dared.
To reach beyond, to touch the sky,
In endless flight, their spirits high.

Awake, my soul, respond to grace,
In every twirl, find your place.
For in this night, rebirth we seek,
A symphony that whispers weak.

So let us soar on wings of dreams,
In harmony, we find our themes.
Together, we create anew,
The starry night, a boundless view.

Echoes of a Soothing Light

In twilight's hush, the shadows blend,
A gentle glow, our hearts to mend.
Each flicker soft, a tale we weave,
In silken threads, we dare believe.

The lanterns sway, like dreams aglow,
Reflecting warmth where love can grow.
Through echoes sweet, our voices rise,
Illuminated, beneath the skies.

With every step, the night unfolds,
A soothing balm for weary souls.
In shadows held, the hopes take flight,
Guided forth by cherished light.

Whispers in the breeze, they sing,
Embracing joy that night will bring.
A lullaby, sweet and serene,
In this embrace, we find the unseen.

Together we bask, hearts intertwined,
In echoes soft, our dreams aligned.
So linger now, let kindness bloom,
In echoes bright, dispelling gloom.

Illuminated Footsteps

On cobblestones, each step a song,
A path of light where we belong.
With every stride, we chase the dawn,
Through whispered dreams, our hopes are drawn.

The lanterns glow, a guiding hand,
Illuminating all the land.
We walk with grace, our fears set free,
In symphony with destiny.

Soft shadows dance, in moonlight's glow,
A rhythm found in ebb and flow.
Each heartbeat echoes through the night,
As footsteps forge our shared delight.

Through quiet streets and hidden ways,
We seek the joy of brighter days.
With every turn, new stories start,
Illuminated by the heart.

Together we tread, hand in hand,
An odyssey across the land.
In every step, let love ignite,
Illuminated, we conquer night.

Chasing the Vanishing Night

As dawn approaches, shadows flee,
The night retreats, yet still we see.
In every star, a moment caught,
We chase the dreams that life has wrought.

With every breath, the silence fades,
New colors bloom where darkness laid.
Through every whisper, time draws near,
In twilight's grasp, we hold no fear.

The echoes of the night resound,
In shadows cast on sacred ground.
With hearts ablaze, we break the dawn,
Chasing the dreams that linger on.

Where hope ignites, we dare to tread,
In fleeting moments, dreams are fed.
As daylight spills its golden light,
We stand as one, embracing sight.

So let us run, with laughter bright,
Chasing the magic of the night.
For every breath brings forth anew,
A promise where the starlight grew.

Tides of Renewal

Whispers of the ocean's breath,
Embrace the shore with gentle grace.
Each wave brings dreams of rebirth,
A dance of time, a soft embrace.

The sun dips low, the sky ablaze,
As colors blend in twilight's glow.
Life ebbs and flows in endless ways,
A cycle where the heart can grow.

Storms may rage, and shadows chase,
Yet here we stand, resilient still.
With every crest, we find our place,
In all the chaos, hope will fill.

Nature sings her sweet refrain,
In echoes of the tide's retreat.
From ash to bloom, through joy and pain,
We rise anew beneath her feet.

So let the tides of time renew,
Our spirits soar, our hearts unbind.
In every swell, in every hue,
We find the strength to leave behind.

The Dance of Emerging Light

From shadows deep, the dawn does break,
With golden rays that softly play.
Emerging light, awake, awake,
To greet the promise of the day.

Petals stretch and greet the sun,
As colors burst in vibrant hues.
The dance of life has just begun,
Nature's canvas, fresh with views.

A symphony of warmth and cheer,
As whispers of the breeze entice.
In every note, the world draws near,
To join the dance, to pay the price.

Each moment holds a breath divine,
A spark of magic, pure delight.
Together, hearts and souls align,
In this grand waltz of emerging light.

So let us twirl and spin around,
In rhythm with the morning glow.
With open arms, our spirits found,
We'll dance with joy, and let love flow.

Soft Echoes of Daybreak

In the stillness of the morn,
Soft echoes call from far away.
The world awakens, reborn,
As shadows fade, the light holds sway.

Gentle whispers through the trees,
As nature stirs from night's embrace.
With each soft sound, the heart finds ease,
In daybreak's kiss, a tender grace.

Birds greet the sun with joyous song,
Their melodies weave through the air.
In harmony, we all belong,
In this serene and quiet prayer.

With every breath, we learn to see,
The beauty in the world so wide.
Soft echoes frame our legacy,
In daybreak's arms, our hearts abide.

So let us treasure dawn's sweet face,
And hold its light within our soul.
In softest echoes, find our place,
As day unfolds, we are made whole.

Serenade to the Dawn

A serenade beneath the stars,
Where whispers weave through velvet night.
The dawn prepares her ageless bars,
To fill our hearts with pure delight.

With crimson hues and gold so bright,
She plays a tune on skies so blue.
Each note, a promise, pure and light,
Inviting all to start anew.

The world awakens, dreams take flight,
As morning dew reflects the glow.
In nature's arms, we find our sight,
In every breeze, her love will flow.

Each moment sings of what's to come,
A tapestry of warmth and grace.
In every heart, her pulse is strum,
The dawn's embrace, our sacred space.

So join the serenade of day,
With open hearts, we'll rise as one.
Together, let us find our way,
In the sweet light of the sun.

Harvesting Joy

In fields where sunlight glows,
The laughter of children flows.
With hands that gather cheer,
We reap the moments dear.

The fruits of love we share,
In every gleam, a prayer.
Through seasons, hearts entwine,
In joy, our souls align.

A harvest of sweet dreams,
As golden sunlight beams.
With gratitude we sing,
For every joy we bring.

Sculpture of Light

In corners dim, it waits,
A dance of light creates.
Shadows twist and play,
In a sculptor's own ballet.

From stone, the spirit flies,
With every chisel, sighs.
A silhouette of grace,
Reflects the heart's embrace.

Each fragment, bright and bold,
A story to be told.
In glass and wood, pure art,
A masterpiece, the heart.

Melodies of Renewal

The dawn brings soft refrain,
Awakening the grain.
With whispers of the breeze,
Nature sings with ease.

Each note a budding dream,
Life flowing like a stream.
In harmony, we grow,
As seasons start to glow.

A chorus of the trees,
Carries the scent of peace.
In every rustling leaf,
Renewal finds belief.

Threads of Gold

In woven dreams of old,
We find our threads of gold.
With patience, hands design,
A tapestry divine.

Through trials, love holds fast,
With each stitch, shadows cast.
In patterns rich and bright,
Our stories take to flight.

Embroidered paths we trace,
In every time and space.
With threads of hope unspun,
Together, we've just begun.

Flickers of Tomorrow

In twilight's glow, dreams ignite,
Stars awaken, shimmering bright.
Whispers of hope dance in the air,
Tomorrow's promise, beyond compare.

Moments linger, silken threads,
Colouring paths where freedom spreads.
Flickers of chance, softly they sway,
Guiding our steps, lighting the way.

Each heartbeat echoes, a silent call,
Through shadows deep, we rise and fall.
Yet in our stride, resilience blooms,
Growing tall amidst the glooms.

Stories unfold, the past unspun,
Beneath the gaze of the setting sun.
With every dawn, a chance anew,
To paint the world in shades of blue.

So hold the spark, let it shine,
In every moment, intertwine.
With flickers of tomorrow, we chase the light,
Together we journey, hearts taking flight.

New Beginnings in Bloom

In gentle folds of morning dew,
A garden wakes, refreshed and new.
Petals unfold, vibrant and bright,
Reveling in spring's warm light.

Seeds of hope in the fertile ground,
Whispers of change all around.
With every blossom, stories untold,
Of courage forged and paths bold.

The sun graces softly, a tender kiss,
As life awakens to moments of bliss.
In every bud, a dream takes flight,
New beginnings bloom, pure and right.

Through seasons that shift, endure and sway,
Nature teaches us, come what may.
In the silence, a symphony plays,
A celebration of hope in myriad ways.

So let us nurture what's yet to grow,
In new beginnings, let love flow.
In the heart of spring, we find our tune,
A dance of life beneath the moon.

Horizons of Change

The horizon whispers, a beckoning call,
With every sunrise, we stand tall.
Shadows retreat as colors align,
Horizons of change where dreams intertwine.

Waves of the ocean, relentless and bold,
Ebb and flow, new stories unfold.
Across the sky, the clouds do drift,
In the winds of change, our spirits lift.

Mountains may rise, but so do we,
Overcoming the challenges, wild and free.
Embracing the journey, we venture wide,
With hopeful hearts, we take the ride.

Time ticks onward, never to pause,
In every change, a reason to cause.
An invitation to turn the page,
To dance through life, engage the stage.

So here we stand, at the edge of dawn,
With open arms, we carry on.
In horizons of change, our spirits soar,
Together we venture, forevermore.

Lifting the Cloak

In shadows deep, where secrets sleep,
A world awaits, our hearts to keep.
Lifting the cloak, we dare to see,
The beauty hidden, wild and free.

Each veil unfurls, one thread at a time,
Revealing the rhythm, a silent rhyme.
In the embrace of gentle light,
We find our truth, shining bright.

Beneath the surface, the colors blend,
Trails of the past, where we ascend.
With courage born from struggle and strife,
We chase the glimpses of vibrant life.

The weight of doubt begins to fade,
As dreams emerge from the masquerade.
Together we search, hand in hand,
In the magic that stirs in this land.

So breathe in deep, let the moments flow,
In lifting the cloak, let our spirits glow.
With open hearts, we find our way,
In the light of love, forever stay.

The Canvas of the New

With colors bright, the dawn breaks clear,
A world awakens, fresh and near.
Each stroke of life, a tale to weave,
In every moment, we believe.

The canvas stretched, pure and wide,
Invites the dreams we cannot hide.
With hopes like paint, we brush the sky,
Embracing visions as we fly.

Through shades of light and shadows cast,
We find our truth, our future vast.
With every hue, a story grows,
In this masterpiece, our spirit flows.

A splash of joy, a hint of pain,
Together they dance, like sun and rain.
In vivid strokes, we carve our way,
The canvas waits, it's ours today.

So hold the brush, and don't delay,
Each choice we make, a brand new day.
With every heartbeat, colors blend,
The canvas calls, our dreams transcend.

Shadows Fade to Memory

The evening whispers soft goodbyes,
As shadows stretch beneath dark skies.
A fleeting moment, none can hold,
Each memory wrapped in tales untold.

Time slips away, like grains of sand,
Fading echoes in the night so grand.
The past, a ghost, it softly sighs,
In twilight's glow, where silence lies.

Yet in our hearts, the light remains,
The love we shared, through joy and pains.
In every tear, a spark of light,
As shadows wane, we find our sight.

We paint our paths with colors bold,
Transforming shadows into gold.
With each step, we chase the dawn,
Where memories linger, and hope is drawn.

So let the shadows fade away,
Embrace the dawn of a brand new day.
For in the light, we find our way,
In fading whispers, bright dreams stay.

Dances with the Dawn

The morning breaks with gentle grace,
As golden rays begin to trace.
With every light, the world awakes,
In joyous leaps, the heart then quakes.

The sky bursts forth with colors bright,
A canvas splashed with pure delight.
The dance of day, a spark, a song,
In nature's rhythm, we belong.

With every step, we join the play,
As dawn invites us to its ballet.
The morning air, so fresh and sweet,
In this embrace, our souls retreat.

We twirl beneath the sun's warm glow,
In vibrant hues, our spirits flow.
Each moment shared, a cherished strand,
In life's grand dance, we take our stand.

So let us sway with joy, not fear,
In dawn's embrace, our path is clear.
For every day is a chance anew,
To dance with dawn, and skies so blue.

Horizon's Invitation

The horizon calls with whispered dreams,
A world awaits beyond the streams.
With every step, adventures bloom,
Into the vast, where wonders loom.

The rising sun, a golden guide,
Invites our hearts to stretch, to glide.
With open arms, we'll chase the light,
Through valleys low, to mountains bright.

Each path we take, a story penned,
In every corner, friends to lend.
The journey matters, not the goal,
For in each turn, we find our soul.

The winds will sing, the stars will dance,
Each breath a gift, a fleeting chance.
So take a step, with courage new,
The horizon awaits, just for you.

In every shadow, light will creep,
As dreams awaken from their sleep.
So lift your gaze, embrace the view,
For life's horizon beckons you.

Colors of a Hopeful Heart

In dawn's embrace, the colors blend,
Whispers of joy, as shadows mend.
A canvas bright, with dreams reborn,
Each hue a promise of a new dawn.

Golden rays light up the morn,
Painting life where hope is worn.
Through every tear, a color shines,
In every heart, the light defines.

Emerald green, a lush refrain,
Lifting spirits, easing pain.
The gentle blue of skies above,
Wraps us tight in warmth and love.

Violet blooms in fragrant fields,
Conveying strength, the truth it yields.
A tapestry of tales untold,
In colors bold, our hearts unfold.

As colors mix, a new birth starts,
Painting dreams on hopeful hearts.
From darkest nights to daylight's shore,
Each shade a story, leading more.

Horizon's Embrace

Beyond the trees, a world so vast,
Where future waits, and shadows cast.
The sun descends, a fiery gold,
Hiding secrets, stories bold.

With every breath, the winds do sing,
As twilight spreads its wondrous wing.
The horizon calls with whispered lore,
Inviting souls to seek for more.

Crimson skies ablaze with light,
Signal the dance of day and night.
An endless road where hopes align,
In each embrace, our hearts entwine.

The stars emerge, a radiant sea,
Guiding dreams to where they'll be.
In shadows deep, we find our way,
With horizon's charm to lead the day.

So let us chase that glowing line,
Where earth and sky in peace combine.
With open hearts, we journey far,
To find our place beneath the star.

The Spectrum of Solace

In quiet rooms, the colors flow,
A palette soft where dreams may grow.
With strokes of peace, the canvas glows,
In gentle hues, the spirit knows.

Lavender whispers in still air,
A soothing balm, a tender care.
Each shade a balm against the pain,
In every corner, hope will reign.

Turquoise waves lap at the shore,
A reminder of what's to explore.
With every breath, we pause and feel,
The vibrant dance that helps to heal.

Sunset oranges melting gold,
A symphony of stories told.
In each warm glow, we find our peace,
A rich embrace that will not cease.

So let the colors draw us near,
In their embrace, we lose our fear.
A spectrum wide, our spirits soar,
In solace found, we seek for more.

Kindling the Forgotten Flame

In shadows deep, a flicker stirs,
A memory stirs, the heart concurs.
With gentle hands, we fan the spark,
To reignite dreams once left in the dark.

The whisper of hope, a tender breeze,
Inviting warmth with quiet ease.
As flames leap high, our fears retreat,
In its glow, our souls meet.

Through flickering light, we trace the way,
To brighter worlds at close of day.
Each spark a beacon, strong and true,
Kindling dreams that once we knew.

From ashes past, new visions rise,
Illuminating endless skies.
With every pulse, the fire warms,
Kindled heart, through every storm.

So never fear the fading night,
For in the dark, we find our light.
Together, we will stoke the flame,
And in our hearts, it lives the same.

The Colors of Renewal

In springtime's breath, the blooms arise,
A tapestry bright beneath the skies.
Petals of pink, and gold, and blue,
Each color whispers tales anew.

Raindrops dance on thirsty ground,
The echoes of life resound all around.
Fresh scents linger in the air,
Nature's canvas, vibrant and rare.

Soft winds carry a gentle song,
Reminding us all where we belong.
As green returns to every tree,
Hope paints the world so vividly.

Beneath the sun, the shadows play,
In fields of gold, they softly sway.
Together in this sacred space,
Life's palette brings us warm embrace.

With every bloom, a promise made,
In every hue, the fears allayed.
A cycle turns, and so we see,
The colors of renewal, wild and free.

Seeds of Possibility

In the soil, dreams nestled tight,
Beneath the earth, out of sight.
Each tiny seed, a world within,
Holds the power to begin.

Sunlight breaks the morning haze,
Gently waking, setting ablaze.
Roots stretch deep, reaching wide,
In quiet faith, they will decide.

Rainfall whispers soft and clear,
Nourishing hopes that disappear.
With every drop, a promise grows,
A future waits, and life bestows.

As shoots emerge from earthen bed,
New stories form, where none were said.
Fertilized by dreams we sow,
In every heart, the seeds will grow.

With patience found in each new dawn,
The path unfolds, the fears all gone.
In vibrant blooms, our dreams align,
Creating wonders, bright and fine.

Unfolding in the Luminescence

In twilight's glow, the stars awake,
Whispering secrets, softly they break.
A dance of light in the evening sky,
Shadows wane, and dreams can fly.

The moon ascends, a guiding friend,
Each ray a promise, love to send.
With silver threads, the night spins tales,
Of journeys gone and all that prevails.

In quietude, bathed in soft glow,
Hearts awaken to what they know.
Each breath a spark, igniting the night,
Unfolding hope in the gentle light.

With every shimmer, the dark retreats,
Illuminated paths where wonder meets.
The magic lingers in the air,
Where dreams are nurtured with tender care.

In this embrace, we find our way,
Through shadows cast, to brighter days.
The world unfolds, our spirits soar,
In luminescence, forevermore.

Where Shadows Flee

In the dawn's embrace, shadows fade,
As light spills forth, a new parade.
Colors emerge where dark once lay,
Chasing the night, ushering day.

The whispered promise of morning's grace,
Banishing fears from their hiding place.
With every beam that breaks the night,
Hope takes root, igniting the light.

Through rustling leaves, soft breezes hum,
Life awakens, embrace the sun.
In each bright corner, shadows retreat,
In unity, our hearts can meet.

The world is vast, yet small we feel,
In warmth of light, our souls can heal.
With every step, from dark we flee,
Boundless freedom, eternally.

In joyful leaps and laughter's sound,
Where shadows flee, new joys are found.
Together we rise, hand in hand,
Embracing life, a radiant band.

From Gloom to Glow

In shadows deep, where silence dwells,
A flicker sparks, as hope compels.
With every breath, the darkness thaws,
A whisper soft, ignites the cause.

Through trials faced, the spirit mends,
The heart finds strength, and love descends.
From ashes cold, a fire ignites,
Now guiding souls through starry nights.

With every dawn, a chance reborn,
To chase the light, where dreams are worn.
The path ahead, though steep it seems,
Is paved with courage, built on dreams.

In laughter shared, the shadows fade,
In every heart, a gentle braid.
Together strong, we'll brave the storm,
From gloom to glow, our spirits warm.

So take my hand, let's journey on,
The night will pass, and greet the dawn.
With every step, our fears outrun,
In unity, our race is won.

The Rise of Hope

From depths of despair, a soft light gleams,
Awakening souls, igniting dreams.
With every heartbeat, a promise made,
Where once was doubt, now courage laid.

Through valleys low, and mountains high,
Hope whispers gently, do not shy.
For in the dark, it plants its seeds,
Nourished by love, and daring deeds.

In every challenge, a lesson found,
A strength within, so deeply bound.
Together we rise, against the tide,
Embracing grace, with arms open wide.

As dawn breaks forth, our spirits soar,
With each new step, we learn to soar.
In every heart, a song now flows,
Life's tender gift, the rise of hope.

So stand with me, as shadows part,
In unity, we play our part.
Together we weave a tapestry,
Of bright tomorrows, meant to be.

Illuminated Paths

With lanterns bright, we find our way,
Through winding roads, both night and day.
Each step we take, a story spun,
In golden light, our journey's begun.

Through forests dense, and mountains steep,
The paths we tread, our memories keep.
With laughter shared, and tears we shed,
Each moment lived, where hope is fed.

In whispered winds, the secrets flow,
Of dreams we dare, and love we sow.
With every turn, new sights appear,
Illuminated paths, where hearts are near.

As day transforms, the stars align,
Their gentle glow, our souls entwine.
In shared embrace, the night unfolds,
Through illuminated paths, our future molds.

So hand in hand, let's journey forth,
To places bright, and depths of worth.
With hearts ablaze, and spirits free,
We carve our fate, in unity.

Echoes of Disquiet

In the stillness, echoes call,
A haunting sound, where shadows fall.
Whispers carried on the breeze,
Of restless hearts, and distant pleas.

Through corridors of time and space,
The fears persist, a haunting trace.
Yet in the dark, a flicker glows,
A chance to grow, as silence slows.

In moments shared, we face the night,
Through echoes soft, we find our light.
With open hearts, we hear the sound,
Of love that springs from common ground.

For in disquiet, beauty lies,
To rise above, and claim the skies.
With every heartbeat, strength we forge,
United voices, a vibrant surge.

So let us dance, through echoes faint,
In every sorrow, find the saint.
Through shadows thick, we'll stand as one,
In echoes of disquiet, life's begun.

The Symphony Awaits

In halls of silence, music waits,
Notes like whispers, open gates.
Each chord a promise, each rest a sigh,
The symphony beckons, come, don't be shy.

Strings are quivering, eager to play,
The heart beats wildly, lost in the sway.
Fingers dance lightly, creating the spell,
In the world of sound, all is well.

Brass and woodwinds join in the fray,
A tapestry woven, night turns to day.
Melody rises, like a bird in flight,
In the arms of music, everything feels right.

Echoes of laughter, shadows in tune,
Notes drifting gently, under the moon.
The symphony awaits, with open embrace,
A journey of stories in each note's grace.

So hear the call, let your spirit soar,
In the symphony's depths, you'll find so much more.
Together we weave, a chorus of dreams,
In the night's embrace, anything redeems.

Whispers in the Sunlight

Golden rays sweep through the trees,
In this moment, my heart's at ease.
Whispers of warmth upon my skin,
A dance of shadows, the day can begin.

Petals unfold, kissed by the light,
Colors explode, a most wondrous sight.
The breeze carries laughter, soft and low,
In the embrace of sunlight's glow.

Birds sing sweetly, a festival cheer,
Every note lingered, pure and clear.
Nature hums softly, in tune with our hearts,
Whispers of beauty, the day imparts.

Moments collected, like gems in a stream,
In this bright world, we savor the dream.
Under the sun's gaze, worries fade,
In whispers of joy, a memory made.

So let us wander, hand in hand,
Through fields of gold, across the land.
In the sunlight's whispers, let's find our way,
A journey of heartbeats, come what may.

Banishing the Gloom

Shadows linger, heavy and gray,
The weight of silence, night steals the day.
Yet hope flickers, like a candle's glow,
Banishing the gloom, as embers flow.

In the darkest corners, whispers of light,
A song of courage, the heart takes flight.
With every heartbeat, shadows recoil,
In resilience woven, we rise from toil.

A dawn awaits, with colors ablaze,
Chasing away the sorrowful haze.
Together we stand, faces aglow,
In unity's strength, the darkness we throw.

The echoes of laughter, a joyous refrain,
As we lift each other, through struggle and pain.
Banishing the gloom, we break every chain,
In the light of our spirit, hope shall remain.

So gather your dreams, let them take flight,
In the tapestry woven, we find our might.
With hearts intertwining, we weather the storm,
Banishing the gloom, our spirits transform.

Ascending from Mist

From the depths of morning, mist starts to rise,
Veils of wonder, shrouded skies.
Each droplet glistens, a world yet unknown,
In the softness of dawn, we find our own.

Mountains awaken, giants of stone,
Wrapped in whispers, standing alone.
The path is unclear, yet we take a chance,
Ascending from mist, in a daring dance.

Through valleys of silence, we stride with care,
Seeking the sunlight, as we journey there.
With every step taken, we shed the doubt,
Ascending from mist, we learn what it's about.

The horizon beckons, a promise so bright,
Where the earth meets the heavens, we move toward the light.
In the heart of the mist, our spirits ignite,
Ascending from mist, we take to flight.

So embrace the journey, with wonder invest,
In the dance of the dawn, we find our quest.
From the haze of the night, let our dreams transpire,
Ascending from mist, to heights that inspire.

Serendipity in Silhouettes

In shadows cast by fading light,
A dance of dreams takes flight.
Whispers echo through the trees,
As stars awaken on gentle breeze.

Moments lost and found anew,
In every sigh, a secret cue.
Silhouettes that weave and sway,
On paths where night turns into day.

A spark ignites the darkened sky,
With every glance, a soft goodbye.
Embrace the chance entwined with fate,
In twilight's arms, we navigate.

With every turn, a story told,
In shadows rich, in hues of gold.
Serendipity sings its song,
In silhouettes, where we belong.

As dawn breaks through the suff'ring night,
A tapestry of pure delight.
Through whispered dreams, we shall abide,
In moments where our hearts collide.

Renewal in the Quietude

In silence deep, the world stands still,
A tranquil heart, a gentle thrill.
The morning dew on blades of grass,
A fresh beginning, time will pass.

Amidst the calm, a breath of grace,
In quietude, we find our place.
With every thought, a seed is sown,
In sacred hush, roots have grown.

The rustle of leaves, the songs of birds,
Life's soft whispers, unspoken words.
In stillness found, we shed the old,
A tapestry of dreams unfold.

Every heartbeat, a gentle wave,
In quiet moments, we are brave.
Renewal waits in shadows cast,
Embracing time, both slow and fast.

Through whispered hopes, we rise anew,
In spaces bright, in skies so blue.
The quietude shall lead the way,
To brighter dawns and cherished days.

Embracing the Warmth Within

In the stillness of a fading day,
Warmth ignites in a gentle sway.
With every glance, a spark ignites,
A glow that dances, pure delights.

The heart, a hearth where embers gleam,
In shadows' play, we dare to dream.
United by love's tender thread,
In warmth embraced, our fears are shed.

Each touch, a promise that gently binds,
In whispered truths, where hope unwinds.
Lessons learned in a loving glow,
Through every trial, together we grow.

In laughter shared and sorrows borne,
We find the light where love is sworn.
Embracing all that makes us whole,
In warmth we nurture, heart and soul.

As twilight beckons with its song,
We hold each other, where we belong.
In the heart's embrace, we shall find,
A warmth that lingers, intertwined.

The Luminous Resurgence

With dawn emerges a radiant glow,
New life unfolds, in soft tableau.
The world awakens from slumber deep,
As golden rays in silence seep.

In vibrant hues, the day reborn,
A canvas bright, through night now worn.
Luminous blessings dance on air,
A promise made, a love laid bare.

Each heartbeat echoes through the morn,
In shadows cast, we are reborn.
The past may fade like twilight's sigh,
But hope ascends on wings to fly.

With every step, our spirits rise,
In swirling colors, we touch the skies.
The luminous whispers carry forth,
A celebration of self and worth.

As daylight shines, we take our stand,
With open hearts and ready hands.
The resurgence sings a song so sweet,
In life's embrace, we are complete.

Flickers of Hope

In shadows deep, a light does spark,
A whisper soft, ignites the dark.
With each small glimmer, dreams take flight,
Flickers of hope, in the night.

Through storms we sail, on roads unclear,
With hearts aglow, we conquer fear.
Each step we take, towards the flame,
Flickers of hope, in life's great game.

The dawn will break, the night will fade,
A tapestry of light is laid.
In every heart, a flame can grow,
Flickers of hope, forever glow.

So when despair grips tight your soul,
Remember still, you are whole.
With open hands, and hearts that strive,
Flickers of hope, keep dreams alive.

Together we rise, through joy and strife,
In each small spark, we find our life.
And in the dark, let courage show,
Flickers of hope, they gently flow.

Awakening the Heart's Glow

In silence deep, where shadows blend,
A seed of light begins to mend.
Awakening dreams from realms afar,
The heart ignites like a shining star.

With gentle touch, we stir the fire,
Igniting hearts with pure desire.
In every pulse, a rhythm found,
Awakening the heart's soft sound.

Through weary paths, we find our grace,
Embracing love in every face.
In laughter shared, and tears we know,
Awakening the heart's warm glow.

In moments lost, and times we dare,
We meet the light, with hearts laid bare.
In unity, our spirits flow,
Awakening the heart's bright glow.

So let us dance, and let us sing,
With each new dawn, our souls take wing.
In every corner, let love grow,
Awakening the heart's sweet glow.

Fragments of a Brighter Tomorrow

In pieces scattered on the ground,
We gather hope, where dreams are found.
Each fragment shines, with stories told,
Fragments of a brighter tomorrow, bold.

Through trials faced, we learn to mend,
With every step, the curves we bend.
In unity, our voices soar,
Fragments of a brighter tomorrow, we explore.

With hands entwined, we lift our gaze,
To vibrant skies, and golden rays.
In every heart, a wish to grow,
Fragments of a brighter tomorrow, we sow.

Each tear we shed, a lesson learned,
In love's warm grip, our souls are turned.
And in the fight, we find our glow,
Fragments of a brighter tomorrow, in flow.

Together we rise, through storms and sun,
In shared resolve, we are made one.
In every heartbeat, let kindness show,
Fragments of a brighter tomorrow, we know.

Constellations of Promise

In the vastness of the night, we see,
Constellations twinkling, wild and free.
Each star a promise, a dream so near,
Constellations of promise, true and clear.

Through cosmic dance, our spirits rise,
In every heart, a spark that flies.
With every wish, we cast our glow,
Constellations of promise, ever flow.

In unity, as galaxies blend,
We find the strength that love can send.
Through distant shores, our hearts will go,
Constellations of promise, ebb and flow.

So let us dream beneath the sky,
With open arms, together we fly.
In every heartbeat, let it show,
Constellations of promise, brightly glow.

In every night, we find our fate,
With every star, we navigate.
In harmony, let our feelings grow,
Constellations of promise, always know.

Resplendent Returns

In the dawn's soft embrace, light unfurls,
Whispers of hope in the air swirl.
Promises made in the night's cool veil,
Resplendent returns, a timeless tale.

The stars fade slowly, surrendering grace,
Shadows retreat, leaving no trace.
A symphony rises as colors bloom,
Filling the world with sweet perfume.

In every heart, a spark ignites,
Painting dreams in the endless nights.
With laughter and love, we dance and play,
Embracing the magic of a new day.

Golden hues bathe the hills so bright,
Chasing away all remnants of night.
Nature awakens, vibrant and bold,
A story of warmth, forever told.

Under the sky where the sun ascends,
Friendships bloom, and the journey bends.
In laughter's echo, we find our song,
In resplendent returns, where we belong.

The Art of Radiance

In shadows deep, a spark ignites,
Crafting dreams on canvas bright.
With every stroke, the colors blend,
The art of radiance, a timeless trend.

Brush against the twilight's kiss,
Creating moments we won't miss.
Whispers of joy in the gentle light,
A masterpiece born from every night.

From dawn to dusk, the palette glows,
In radiant hues, the spirit flows.
Hearts connected in this beautiful dance,
Embracing the magic, seizing the chance.

Each heartbeat paints a tale to tell,
In the gallery where memories dwell.
With laughter as colors, and love the frame,
The art of radiance, never the same.

So let us wander through vibrant days,
Creating beauty in countless ways.
In each moment, let us find,
The brilliance captured in heart and mind.

Beyond the Night's Grasp

When the stars whisper secrets rare,
And dreams take flight on gentle air.
Beyond the night, where shadows cease,
A dawn approaches, bringing peace.

In twilight's hold, the world stands still,
With hushed breaths and a tranquil thrill.
Each moment lingers, suspended in time,
A melody soft as a distant chime.

The moon's embrace, a guiding light,
Leading us through the velvet night.
With hope aglow and spirits free,
We wander forth, you and me.

In the horizon's blush, we find our way,
Breaking the chains of yesterday.
With open hearts, we rise and soar,
Beyond the night's grasp, forevermore.

Each heartbeat echoes, a promise made,
In the silent vows, love won't fade.
Together we'll journey, hand in hand,
To the dawn's embrace, a radiant land.

Sculpting Optimal Paths

In the garden of dreams, we lay our roots,
Sculpting optimal paths in pursuit of truths.
With each step taken, we shape our way,
Crafting our futures, come what may.

Through winding trails, we learn and grow,
Learning to dance in the ebb and flow.
With every stumble, we find our grace,
Sculpting our lives as we navigate space.

The map of our hearts, drawn with care,
Guiding our feet through despair and fare.
In every choice, possibilities gleam,
Revealing the power of our shared dream.

As we journey forth, hand in hand,
Building together, a world so grand.
With courage and love, we'll find our way,
Sculpting optimal paths, day by day.

In unity's strength, our spirits combine,
Creating a legacy, pure and divine.
With kindness as compass, together we flow,
Sculpting the life that continues to grow.

Notes of Resurgence

In shadows deep, a melody sings,
Hope rising like the dawn of spring.
Each note a promise, whispers of grace,
Resurgence blooms in time and space.

Faint echoes linger, softly they play,
Filling hearts with warmth each day.
Through trials faced, we find the song,
A symphony where we belong.

With every chord, the past unfolds,
In every silence, a truth retolds.
Together we lift our voices high,
A chorus that cannot die.

From ashes deemed, the fire ignites,
Desires ignited, soaring heights.
Resurgence blooms, a tale reborn,
In the heart of night, there's a new dawn.

Through stormy seas, we find our way,
The notes of life, they lead and sway.
Each struggle faced, a step to rise,
In every heart, the future lies.

Unseen Brighter Days

Beyond the clouds, the sun still shines,
With whispered winds, hope intertwines.
Though shadows linger, light breaks through,
In unseen days, the world feels new.

A tapestry woven with threads of gold,
Stories of warmth yet to be told.
Each step we take, the path reveals,
Brighter days, a fate that heals.

Fragments of dreams in twilight's embrace,
Guiding us gently through time and space.
In the hush of night, our hearts will sway,
To the rhythm of unseen brighter days.

With courage found in quiet grace,
We navigate through every space.
Hand in hand, we rise and roam,
Unseen days lead us back home.

Embers of hope illuminate the night,
A beacon of trust, forever bright.
Together we seek, in unity play,
A future painted with brighter days.

Steps Toward the Luminous

With every breath, we seek the light,
In sacred moments, heart takes flight.
Each step a dance toward the divine,
Paths converge where stars align.

In whispered dreams, the visions glow,
Leading us onward, helping us grow.
Through shadows cast, a beacon shines,
Steps toward the luminous, love entwines.

In the stillness, we find our way,
Guided by hope, come what may.
With faith ablaze, we break the night,
In each step taken, we find the light.

Mountains high, the valleys low,
In every journey, truths will flow.
With hearts as one, we journey far,
Steps toward the luminous, chasing stars.

Together we rise, unafraid to dream,
Bound by the light, a radiant beam.
In love's embrace, we find our grace,
Steps toward the luminous, we embrace.

A Light Beyond Reason

In the depths of night, a flicker glows,
A light beyond reason, where hope flows.
Through darkest fears, it starts to rise,
Guiding our hearts, a sweet disguise.

In the maze of thoughts, we lose our way,
Yet this light whispers, 'look and stay.'
With eyes closed tight, we seek the truth,
In love's warm light, we find our youth.

Moments drift like leaves in air,
But this light beckons, always there.
Beyond the noise, a stillness waits,
A light that opens all the gates.

In calm surrender, we learn to see,
The light beyond reason, setting us free.
With gentle hands, it heals our soul,
Reminding us, we are whole.

As stars align, our spirits soar,
A dance of light, forevermore.
In unity found, we dare to believe,
A light beyond reason, we shall achieve.

Embracing the Dawn

Soft whispers break the night,
A canvas brushed with gold,
The sun begins its flight,
As dreams and hopes unfold.

Morning dew on petals gleam,
Nature stirs from sleep,
A world that starts to dream,
In colors bright and deep.

Birds sing a joyful tune,
A symphony of light,
The warmth of sun at noon,
Makes shadows take to flight.

Every heartbeat quickens pace,
As shadows dance away,
With every tender trace,
We greet the brand new day.

In this moment, breathe in deep,
Feel the warmth so near,
Embrace the dawn, and keep,
The light forever clear.

The Promise of Tomorrow

Stars twinkle in the gloom,
Whispers of hope arise,
A future to consume,
Beneath the endless skies.

Paths not yet defined,
Lies an adventure bold,
With dreams intertwined,
A story yet untold.

Through trials we will tread,
With courage in our hearts,
Onward we will be led,
As the new day departs.

Each step a vow we make,
To cherish and to strive,
For every dream we wake,
In the light, we will thrive.

With every dawn we share,
A promise to renew,
In life's intricate care,
Tomorrow starts with you.

Singing in the Light

Radiance fills the air,
Gold streams through the trees,
A melody to share,
Carried on the breeze.

Voices rise in delight,
As shadows fall away,
Together we ignite,
The warmth of yesterday.

Sunlight dances on streams,
Waves of laughter flow,
Chasing all our dreams,
With a radiant glow.

In the stillness of morning,
Life's promises unfold,
A new day affirming,
In hues of red and gold.

Underneath the wide sky,
We find our hearts unite,
With joy, we shall not lie,
Forever singing bright.

Reclaiming the Day

The night was filled with fears,
But dawn brings calm and peace,
With sunlight drying tears,
We seek a lighted lease.

Awakening our souls,
We rise to take our stand,
To mend what time consoles,
And craft a brighter land.

With every breath we take,
We write a brand new tale,
A promise we will make,
Where love will never fail.

In unity, we gather,
With hope that brightly shines,
For every heart that flutters,
In rhythm as it aligns.

Reclaiming what is ours,
With strength in every way,
Together, we are stars,
In this vibrant display.

A Tapestry of Glimmers

Threads of light weave through the dark,
In whispers soft like a lark.
Colors blend in a gentle swirl,
A tapestry of dreams unfurl.

Moments captured in amber hue,
Secrets whispered, old and new.
Each glimmer tells a story bright,
A dance of shadows, a spark of light.

Patterns form in the twilight sky,
As the stars prepare to fly.
With every twinkle, hope ignites,
A symphony of endless lights.

From the canvas of the night,
Emerge visions, pure delight.
We wander through this woven dream,
Where nothing's ever as it seems.

In the stillness, hearts align,
As the glimmers intertwine.
Together, they create and weave,
A world where we can believe.

Rising from the Ashen Gloom

From the depths of dark despair,
Hope begins to fill the air.
Emerging from the smoky veil,
A vision rises, fierce and pale.

The embers flicker in the void,
A heart once broken, now employed.
Strength unfolds like wings anew,
Transforming fears as they break through.

With each breath, the shadows fade,
In silence, courage is remade.
The dawn ignites the barren land,
A promise held in tender hand.

Lessons learned in fire's embrace,
Resilience blooms, finds its place.
From ashes black, a spirit born,
A new beginning, softly worn.

In the glare of rising light,
Every soul will take flight.
Through the gloom, we find our way,
Into the warmth of a new day.

The Path to Radiance

Through the forest, soft and deep,
Where secrets weave and shadows creep.
A winding trail begins to show,
With whispers sweet and winds that blow.

Each step holds promise, bright and clear,
The laughter of the leaves we hear.
In every turn, a glimmer waits,
Leading us to open gates.

The branches sway, a graceful dance,
Inviting us to take a chance.
With every heartbeat, every glance,
We find our dreams in nature's trance.

Up ahead, the sunlight breaks,
A golden bridge where the heart awakes.
In radiant glow, we learn to see,
The true essence of being free.

As we walk this path we've sought,
Warmth of hope is gently caught.
Together, hand in hand we stride,
On this journey, side by side.

Sunbeams on the Horizon

Morning breaks with hues divine,
As sunbeams dance on edges fine.
A canvas bright, each ray a brush,
Bringing life in a golden hush.

Upon the fields, a gentle glow,
Awakens dreams from sleep below.
Nature stirs, the world will rise,
In the warmth of painted skies.

Every step feels light and free,
Inspired by the light we see.
With laughter running through the air,
We celebrate, we strip bare.

Sun-kissed moments, sweet embrace,
Filling hearts with endless grace.
In the warmth, we feel alive,
With each ray, our spirits thrive.

As day unfolds with gentle ease,
We find our strength, we find our peace.
The horizon calls, a bright refrain,
With sunbeams dancing, we remain.

The Symphony of New Beginnings

In the dawn of a fresh new day,
Hope awakens, leading the way.
Seeds of dreams break through the soil,
With each heartbeat, we begin to toil.

Notes of laughter fill the air,
Every moment, a chance to dare.
Chasing shadows of yesterday,
We embrace the light, come what may.

Buds of courage start to bloom,
Casting aside the weight of gloom.
With every step, we rise anew,
A symphony, just me and you.

Let the past dissolve in time,
As we climb together, we chime.
Voices join, a chorus bold,
In every story, love unfolds.

Together, we will pave the path,
Defy the storms, endure the wrath.
In union, we craft our own song,
The symphony where we belong.

Palette of the Morning Sky

The horizon blushes, paints a scene,
With strokes of gold, and hues of green.
Clouds whisper secrets in twilight's grace,
A masterpiece, nature's sweet embrace.

Shimmers of pink, and splashes of blue,
Each dawn brings a promise, fresh and new.
Brush of the sun on the canvas wide,
The palette dances, our hearts abide.

Birds take flight on a canvas bright,
Chasing the colors that feel so right.
With every shade, a story's spun,
Awakening dreams as bright as the sun.

In this gallery of endless views,
The morning sings, each note imbues.
Colorful whispers soar and glide,
In the palette, our hopes reside.

As day unfolds, we'll hold it dear,
The beauty of moments, crystal clear.
In every sunrise, love takes its stand,
A vibrant masterpiece, hand in hand.

Caress of a Gentle Breeze

Whispers float on the evening air,
A soft embrace, without a care.
Leaves sway slowly, dancing low,
In the gentle breeze, our hearts will flow.

It carries scents of blooms in spring,
A tender touch, like love's first fling.
Through fields of gold, it sweeps so light,
Bringing warmth on a chilly night.

With each sigh, the night comes alive,
In the caress, our spirits thrive.
It takes our worries, sends them away,
In the fading light of the day.

Every rustle tells a tale,
Of memories shared, of dreams that sail.
On the wings of whispers, we are free,
Lost in the magic, just you and me.

With every breath, we find our peace,
In the gentle breeze, our sorrows cease.
Together we sway, in nature's song,
In this embrace, where we belong.

Light Dancing on Water

Ripples shimmer in a tranquil bay,
As the sun stretches at the end of day.
Golden glimmers, playful and bright,
A graceful dance in the soft twilight.

Waves caress the silken shore,
Each reflection opens a door.
Shadows blend in a liquid grace,
Light joins water in a serene embrace.

The world fades as time stands still,
In this dance, our hearts we thrill.
Nature's mirror holds our gaze,
In this magic, we drift, we blaze.

Every twinkle tells a story deep,
Of dreams held close, of promises we keep.
As the moon rises, the light will change,
Yet in our hearts, it feels so strange.

With every ripple, our spirits soar,
In the dance of light, we crave for more.
The water sparkles, a vibrant song,
Together in this moment, we belong.

In the Wake of Fading Shadows

Whispers of night, they gently fade,
Starlit memories, softly laid.
Echoes linger in the dim,
As dreams dance quiet, sweet and slim.

Moonlight spills on the cold ground,
Wrapping silence all around.
Fading shadows stretch and creep,
In this twilight, secrets we keep.

Crescent smiles on the horizon,
Promise of dawn, a new season.
With every breath, hope ignites,
Chasing away the darkest nights.

Gentle breezes kiss the trees,
Whispers carried on the breeze.
In the calm, peace takes its hold,
As night drapes in silvers and gold.

Stars retreat, their light now dim,
The dawn beckons, sweet and slim.
In the wake of shadows cast,
We rise anew, free at last.

A Canvas of New Horizons

Brush of colors on the sky,
Where dreams and wishes soar high.
Each stroke tells a story bright,
Painting hopes in morning light.

Mountains stand, strong and bold,
In their shadows, tales unfold.
Rivers carve paths, wild and free,
Guiding hearts to destiny.

Fields of gold sway in the sun,
Whispering songs of work well done.
Every grain tells of the past,
A future bright, built to last.

Clouds drift lazily, shades and hues,
An artist's palette, bright and true.
Each season brings a chance to shine,
In every moment, a spark divine.

On this canvas, life unfolds,
With each heartbeat, love holds.
A tapestry woven rich and grand,
In every shade, we take a stand.

From Gloom to Glimmer

In the depths, where shadows lie,
Whispers of hope begin to sigh.
Each tear a pearl, a lesson learned,
From gloom to glimmer, hearts have turned.

Silent cries in the darkest hour,
Yet within, lies hidden power.
A flicker, a spark, ignites the soul,
Leading us out, making us whole.

Morning breaks with gentle light,
Chasing away the remnants of night.
With every dawn, a chance to rise,
With courage found in the skies.

Softly rises the warm sun,
Painting skies, a new day begun.
In every shadow, courage found,
A glimmer of hope, tightly bound.

From despair to joy, we weave,
In every heart, a way to believe.
Though storms may come, we will endure,
From gloom to glimmer, we are sure.

Crescendo of the Rising Sun

In the stillness, silence hums,
A beat of life as morning comes.
Colors burst, the sky ignites,
A symphony of day and night.

Notes of dawn lift spirits high,
As shadows flee and dreams comply.
Crescendo swells in vibrant hues,
With every breath, the day renews.

Waves of gold wash o'er the land,
Nature's touch, a tender hand.
In each ray, a story spun,
The promise of a day begun.

Birds take flight, a joyous call,
Echoing the hope for all.
In this moment, hearts align,
As daybreak brings a bright design.

With each heartbeat, life's refrain,
Resilient spirit, free from pain.
In this crescendo, we find our way,
To embrace the gifts of the day.

A New Chapter Unfolds

Turning the page, fresh and bright,
New dreams awaken, taking flight.
With courage, we face the unknown,
In every heartbeat, new seeds are sown.

Step by step, we forge ahead,
Writing stories yet to be said.
Each word a brushstroke, bold and clear,
Painting visions we hold dear.

The past a whisper, soft and light,
Guiding us gently towards the light.
In this moment, we embrace change,
A tapestry woven, vibrant and strange.

With every choice, we redefine,
Celebrating the paths that intertwine.
A symphony of voices begins to sing,
In unity, we find the strength to bring.

Together we rise, a brand-new start,
Crafting a future, each plays a part.
In the journey of life, we will behold,
A new chapter unfolds, adventures untold.

The Splendor of Rejuvenation

In the quiet dawn, life starts anew,
Nature awakens with vibrant hue.
Blossoms unfurl in the soft spring air,
Each petal whispers, beauty laid bare.

Streams flow gently, crystals aglow,
Carving the earth with grace and flow.
The sun graces us with warming light,
A canvas painted, pure and bright.

Birds take to wing with songs of cheer,
Each melody ringing, crystal clear.
The world rejoices in laughter's embrace,
We cherish the magic of time and space.

The trees stand tall, proud and free,
Guardians of secrets, of ancient glee.
In harmony, life dances and spins,
Where every beginning, a chance to begin.

With every heartbeat, life is reborn,
In the splendor of dawn, a new story is sworn.
In the embrace of change, we rediscover,
The beauty within, like no other.

Threads of Golden Promise

Woven together with strands of hope,
Life's tapestry forms with every slope.
Each thread a story, unique and bold,
In the fabric of time, treasures untold.

Colors entwine, such vibrant grace,
In the loom of existence, we find our place.
Through struggles and triumphs, we stitch and seam,
Creating a quilt born from a dream.

Golden promises shimmer and shine,
In the heart's embrace, forever entwine.
We gather the moments, both small and grand,
Crafting a legacy with loving hands.

A journey unfolds, each step adorned,
With hope in our hearts, we're reborn.
In the language of life, we weave and bend,
Threads of connection that never end.

Together we rise, hand in hand,
In this vast tapestry, we take a stand.
With every stitch, let futures align,
In the threads of promise, our dreams intertwine.

Unfurling Wings at Daylight

As dawn breaks soft, a hush descends,
Awakening dreams that the night defends.
With a breath, the world stirs awake,
Unfurling wings, a journey to take.

In the light of morn, we stretch and yawn,
Chasing the shadows, embracing the dawn.
With every pulse, the heart takes flight,
In the magic of morning, everything feels right.

Nature unfurls in colors so bright,
A canvas of hope, a dazzling sight.
With every whisper, the breeze invites,
To dance in the glow of new delights.

The sky adorned with hues of gold,
Stories of freedom yet to be told.
Each bird a symbol of dreams set free,
In the symphony of life, we find harmony.

Together we rise, the day is ours,
Beneath the blanket of twinkling stars.
With courage ignited, let spirits soar,
Unfurling wings, we embrace what's in store.

The Healing Palette

In shades of green, the leaves embrace,
Soft whispers wrap in nature's grace.
Brushstrokes gentle, tender and true,
Hearts uplifted beneath skies blue.

Colors blend in a vibrant dance,
Hope ignites with every chance.
The canvas waits with eager hands,
As healing flows across the lands.

With each new hue, a story grows,
A tapestry of joy that glows.
Soft pastels cradle weary dreams,
Within this wonder, light redeems.

A palette nourished by sun and rain,
Embracing beauty born from pain.
Each color sings, a siren's call,
Together we rise, united all.

In the quiet, colors entwine,
Creating peace as hearts align.
The healing palette spreads its wings,
In every stroke, the heart now sings.

Breathe in the Radiance

Breathe in the radiance of dawn's first light,
Awake the soul from the grips of night.
Each moment glimmers, a brand new start,
Inhaling joy that fills the heart.

Colors swirl in the rising sun,
Whispers of warmth that have just begun.
Inhale the beauty that nature yields,
Exhale doubt in the blooming fields.

Let the brilliance wash over your skin,
Feel the magic that comes from within.
Every breath a dance, every sigh a song,
Together we flourish, where we belong.

The breeze carries tales of love and peace,
In this embrace, let worries cease.
Breathe in the radiance, let it fill,
Each moment cherished, a heart to thrill.

As sunlight kisses the earth below,
We find our courage and let it grow.
With every inhale, we claim our space,
Inhale the wonder, exhale the grace.

Rising from the Ashes

From the ashes, a phoenix takes flight,
A symbol of hope in the darkest night.
Fires may burn, but life will return,
In the heart of struggle, we learn to yearn.

With each ember, a story unfolds,
In every wound, the spirit molds.
Courage ignited, resilience shines,
From barren ground, the wildflower climbs.

The heat of trials stirs dormant seeds,
Life emerging from powerful needs.
As shadows fade, vibrant colors bloom,
In the garden of dreams, dispelling gloom.

Rise from the ashes, embrace the glow,
A dance of rebirth in the ebb and flow.
The spirit soars on renewed wings,
In the heart of chaos, a new song sings.

With every sunrise, hope is reborn,
A testament bright that love can adorn.
From the ashes, a promise takes shape,
In the strength of our hearts, we learn to escape.

A Symphony of New Light

In the dawn's embrace, the world awakes,
A symphony formed as daylight breaks.
Nature joins in with a joyous cheer,
Each note a promise, echoing clear.

The sky plays hues of gold and blue,
A canvas alive, painted fresh and true.
Trees sway gently to nature's refrain,
In every whisper, love's song contains.

Birds take flight in a harmonious quest,
Carving the air with beauty expressed.
The melody swells, embracing the day,
Guiding our hearts in a wondrous play.

Light dances softly on rippling streams,
Illuminating hopes, igniting dreams.
In the stillness, vibrant spirits unite,
Together we flourish, a radiant sight.

In this symphony, joy intertwines,
With every heartbeat, the universe shines.
Let us revel in this aura so bright,
For we are the music, a chorus of light.

Milton Keynes UK
Ingram Content Group UK Ltd.
UKHW021929011224
451790UK00005B/84